How to Form a Lasting Love Relationship

How to Form a Lasting Love Relationship

Dr. Lowell D. Rosman
Dr. Samuel A. Feldman
Dr. Howard Rosenberg

COMPACT BOOKS

Library of Congress Cataloging in Publication Data

Rosman, Lowell D.
  How to form a lasting love relationship!

  Bibliography: p.
  Includes index.
  1. Interpersonal relations.   2. Love.   I. Feldman,
Samuel A.   II. Rosenberg, Howard, 1942–
III. Title.
HM132.R665   1986   158′.2   86-4200
ISBN 0-936320-24-9 (pbk.)

Contents

To those who have helped us appreciate loving relationships--our wives, parents, children, teachers, patients, students, friends and colleagues.

The authors also acknowledge the role of Mark Rosman in compiling this book.

About the Authors

DR. LOWELL D. ROSMAN is a Diplomate, American Boarcd of Psychiatry and Nuerology and Diplomate, American Board of Child Psychiatry. Dr. Rosman holds the position of Assistant Clinical Professor of Psychiatry, University of Miami Medical School and Southeastern College of Osteopathic Medicine, Miami, FL. In addition, he maintains a private practice in psychiatry with children, adolescents and adults. He has written several articles and contributed his views through radio and TV appearances, as well as through professional projects. He has been an active member in the American Psychiatric Association, Florida Psychiatric Association, and the Dade County Mental Health Association. Dr. Rosman has been married 27 years and has two children.

DR. SAMUEL A. FELDMAN is a Clinical Psychologist in full time private practice. He has held the position of professor, Miami Dade Community College, Miami, Florida. Dr. Feldman has worked for the past 25 years in the areas of marriage and family counseling, child abuse, delinquency and psychodiagnostic testing, and serves as a court-appointed psychologist for marital and custody-contested cases of the circuit court, Miami, Florida. He has been an active member of the American Association of Psychiatric clinics for children, American Psychological Association, Dade County Psychological Association, and the Dade County Mental Health Association. He served as an advisor to Parents Without Partners, is a founding member of the American Psychology Law Society, and was a founder of the Dade County Juvenile Psychiatric Clinic. Dr. Feldman has been married 20 years and has two children.

DR. HOWARD ROSENBERG holds the position of Associate Professor, Florida International University, where he has been a full-time faculty member for the past 10 years. He has written numerous professional journal articles, several test instruments, and has presented papers at international, national and regional professional conferences. He has been an active member in the American Psychological Association, National Vocational Guidance Association, American Association for Counseling and Development, and the National Rahabilitation Association. He is a licensed School Psychologist, State of Florida, and a certified School Psycholgist, State of New York. Dr. Rosenberg has worked with disabled individuals and their families for the past 20 years in the areas of psychodiagnostic testing, marriage and family counseling, and personal, social and vocational adjustment counseling. Dr. Rosenberg has been married for 13 years and has one child.

Introduction

Imprinted somewhere in the mind of virtually every person is the true Great American Dream: to grow up, find and marry someone you truly love and who truly loves you, and live happily ever after, sharing that joyous love with your children.

Unfortunately, for too many people, the Great American Dream is turning into a nightmare. The divorce rate is at an astounding 50% percent, meaning that every other marriage is doomed to failure. Certainly, the two individuals who are divorcing aren't the only victims. The children are just as much traumatized by the breakup as the parents. Society, too, is as much a victim since the very existence of the nuclear family is being threatened.

Besides the very real and immediate emotional and pyschic pain caused by divorce, we now recognize a much more potent, much more debilitating side-effect of the poor state of disrepair of marriage in this country: the growing difficulty for individuals--even those who have never been married and have not experienced the anxiety caused by divorce--to enter into and nurture successful lasting love relationships.

This new, worrisome social phenomenon has its roots in many areas: individuals, fully cognizant of the failure rate of marriages, shy away from the institution, not wanting to suffer the anxiety of a divorce; children of divorced parents recall the turmoil of their parent's marriage and recoil at the thought of reliving that vividly-painful experience; and many individuals who have unsuccessfully tried to find a lasting love mate, finally throw their hands up in despair, and decide marriage is not for them.

Complicating the situation is the fact that no one is taught how to select a mate; instead, we tend to base the most important decision of our lives on pure emotional and physical attraction, seeking the "chemistry" so often talked about, but seldom found.

Yet, we have developed a system of self-understanding--and understanding of potential partners--that will help you find a mate with whom you can share a lasting love relationship. Don't worry if your past social record has been a series of dating the wrong type--this book will help you identify the inner workings that attracted you to the wrong type of person, and allow you to rewrite your inner guidelines to select potential mates who are good for you, and who have the ability to nurture and love you.

This book is unlike others, because it requires more than your reading; it also demands your participation. For example, four identical questionnaires are contained in the text--the first two follow this introduction, the last two are located at the end of the book. Please take a moment now to complete the first two questionnaires before you begin reading the book. After you've completed the book, finish the last two questionnaires. The difference in your answers--which will come as a result of your new understanding of yourself, and what type of mate is ideal for you, will surprise you.

At the end of each chapter is a blank page entitled, "My Thoughts and Feelings About This Chapter." This page provides you, the reader, with the opportunity to crystalize what you have learned from the chapter. These notations can be used later on when you are ready to complete the second set of questionnaires at the end of the book.

What ever happened to happily-ever-after? The new method proposed in this book may help you find the answer. We wish you well.

About The Questionnaires

    The following two questionnaires should be filled out by you. By evaluating your own personality qualities and the qualities of your potential partner, you will be further prepared for a long lasting love relationship. The ten main categories have been found to be critical components in positive interpersonal relationships. These ten categroies should be evaluated by rating each item withing the category (total of 70) and then rating each category as a whole. The key issue to keep in mind is the "goodness of the fit" between you and your patner.

    Hence, the potential for a long lasting love relationship would be indicated by a very good or outstanding "fit" between you and your partner. The acceptable areas would require a good deal of inner work. When the absence of "fit" is indicated by a preponderance of unacceptable ratings, the potential for a long lasting relationship is minimal.

    Place a check in the appropriate rating category for each item within the ten personality categories, as well as for each category itself. You may write out in narrative form on the questionnaire's back side why you rated the quality as either unacceptable, acceptable, very good or outstanding. By writing out your explanations, you will be able to better discuss the personality qualities with either your potential partner or any other person. It is important to share similarities with your potential partner in order to establish a fulfilling relationship. Obviously, no one partner can meet all the needs of another, but the more areas of agreement, the higher the potential for a lasting relationship.

I. PRE-TEST—SELF EVALUATION

PERSONALITY QUALITIES

RATING SCALE

I. Self-Esteem

	outstanding	very good	acceptable	unacceptable
1. Ability to take a stand on a controversial issue				
2. Willingness to take risks and experience possible failure				
3. Belief in your potential for success in achieving goals				
4. Ability to appreciate your accomplishments without convincing others of your achievements				
5. Ability to recongize your strengths				
6. Ability to accept limitations				
7. Willingness to recognize and strenthen weaknesses				
8. Ability to be resilient after failure				
9. Degree of self-reliance and self confidence				
10. Willingness to seek assistance when necessary				
11. Confidence in your decisions				
12. Awareness of physical appearance				

I. PRE-TEST—SELF EVALUATION

PERSONALITY QUALITIES

RATING SCALE

	outstanding	very good	acceptable	unacceptable
II. Communication/Openess				
13. Ability to voice a complaint without feeling self-conscious				
14. Ability to accept a complaint without considering it a personal affront				
15. Willingess and ability to share feelings and thoughts				
16. Ability to display warmth				
17. Ability to try new experiences				
III. Empathy/Sensitivity				
18. Ability to participate in a reciprocal relationship				
19. Respect for the needs of others				
20. Ability to identify your own views				
21. Ability to admit you're wrong				
22. Willingness to listen attentively to others and offer feedback				
23. Ability to put yourself in the position of another				
24. Willingness to accept others as they are, and not try to change their "bad" ways				

I. PRE-TEST—SELF EVALUATION

PERSONALITY QUALITIES

RATING SCALE

	outstanding	very good	acceptable	unacceptable
IV. Social Responsiveness				
25. Accepting responsibility for your own actions				
26. Ability to get along with others				
27. Social manners				
28. Quality of friends of the same sex				
29. Acceptance of your social role and responsibility				
30. Ability to maintain career goals				
V. Control				
31. Moderation in general demeanor				
32. Ability to accept criticism without losing your temper				
33. Self-discipline				
34. Ability to delay impulse gratification				
35. High tolerance of frustration				
36. Capacity to plan for the future				
VI. Predominant Mood				
37. Ability to work at high-energy levels when necessary				
38. Ability to maintain an even disposition/exhibit patience				

I. PRE-TEST—SELF EVALUATION

PERSONALITY QUALITIES

RATING SCALE

	outstanding	very good	acceptable	unacceptable
39. Enthusiasm/spontaneity				
40. Predictable behavior patterns				
41. Ability to avoid sulking after disappointment				
VII. Affection/Sexuality				
42. Warmth in sexual expression				
43. Enjoy physical touching				
44. Enjoy giving sexual satisfaction				
45. Enjoy receiving sexual satisfaction				
46. Does not rush sexuality				
47. Views sexual compatability as important				
48. Ability to delay self-gratification				
VIII. Trustworthiness				
49. Loyalty to family and friends				
50. Consistency in fulfilling commitments				
51. Ability to keep your word				
52. Consider sexual fidelity important				
53. Reliable				
54. Keeps appointments				

I. PRE-TEST—SELF EVALUATION

PERSONALITY QUALITIES

RATING SCALE

	outstanding	very good	acceptable	unacceptable

IX. Social Compatability

55. Share recreational interests
56. Share moral beliefs
57. Similar cultural values
58. Ability to strike a balance between work/personal life
59. Share religious beliefs/respect view of others
60. Common socio-economic goals
61. Sense of humor
62. Similar career directions
63. Accpetance of partner by family

X. Interdependence/ Equalitarianism

64. Encourages mutual decision making
65. Balance between dependence/independence
66. Ability to rely on others, as well as on self
67. Ability to enjoy the company of others
68. Ability to tolerate being alone with no undue stress

I. PRE-TEST—SELF EVALUATION

PERSONALITY QUALITIES

69. Ability to sustain friendships

70. Ability to accept leadership role, or subordinate role, when appropriate

RATING SCALE

outstanding	very good	acceptable	unacceptable

II. PRE-TEST—EVALUATION OF PARTNER

PERSONALITY QUALITIES

RATING SCALE

I. Self-Esteem

	outstanding	very good	acceptable	unacceptable
1. Ability to take a stand on a controversial issue				
2. Willingness to take risks and experience possible failure				
3. Belief in your potential for success in achieving goals				
4. Ability to appreciate your accomplishments without convincing others of your achievements				
5. Ability to recongize your strengths				
6. Ability to accept limitations				
7. Willingness to recognize and strenthen weaknesses				
8. Ability to be resilient after failure				
9. Degree of self-reliance and self confidence				
10. Willingness to seek assistance when necessary				
11. Confidence in your decisions				
12. Awareness of physical appearance				

II. PRE-TEST—EVALUATION OF PARTNER

PERSONALITY QUALITIES

RATING SCALE

	outstanding	very good	acceptable	unacceptable

II. Communication/Openess

13. Ability to voice a complaint without feeling self-conscious
14. Ability to accept a complaint without considering it a personal affront
15. Willingess and ability to share feelings and thoughts
16. Ability to display warmth
17. Ability to try new experiences

III. Empathy/Sensitivity

18. Ability to participate in a reciprocal relationship
19. Respect for the needs of others
20. Ability to identify your own views
21. Ability to admit you're wrong
22. Willingness to listen attentively to others and offer feedback
23. Ability to put yourself in the position of another
24. Willingness to accept others as they are, and not try to change their "bad" ways

II. PRE-TEST—EVALUATION OF PARTNER

PERSONALITY QUALITIES

RATING SCALE

	outstanding	very good	acceptable	unacceptable
IV. Social Responsiveness				
25. Accepting responsibility for your own actions				
26. Ability to get along with others				
27. Social manners				
28. Quality of friends of the same sex				
29. Acceptance of your social role and responsibility				
30. Ability to maintain career goals				
V. Control				
31. Moderation in general demeanor				
32. Ability to accept criticism without losing your temper				
33. Self-discipline				
34. Ability to delay impulse gratification				
35. High tolerance of frustration				
36. Capacity to plan for the future				
VI. Predominant Mood				
37. Ability to work at high-energy levels when necessary				
38. Ability to maintain an even disposition/exhibit patience				

II. PRE-TEST—EVALUATION OF PARTNER

PERSONALITY QUALITIES

RATING SCALE

	outstanding	very good	acceptable	unacceptable
39. Enthusiasm/spontaneity				
40. Predictable behavior patterns				
41. Ability to avoid sulking after disappointment				

VII. Affection/Sexuality

	outstanding	very good	acceptable	unacceptable
42. Warmth in sexual expression				
43. Enjoy physical touching				
44. Enjoy giving sexual satisfaction				
45. Enjoy receiving sexual satisfaction				
46. Does not rush sexuality				
47. Views sexual compatability as important				
48. Ability to delay self-gratification				

VIII. Trustworthiness

	outstanding	very good	acceptable	unacceptable
49. Loyalty to family and friends				
50. Consistency in fulfilling commitments				
51. Ability to keep your word				
52. Consider sexual fidelity important				
53. Reliable				
54. Keeps appointments				

II. PRE-TEST—EVALUATION OF PARTNER

PERSONALITY QUALITIES

RATING SCALE

PERSONALITY QUALITIES	outstanding	very good	acceptable	unacceptable
IX. Social Compatability				
55. Share recreational interests				
56. Share moral beliefs				
57. Similar cultural values				
58. Ability to strike a balance between work/personal life				
59. Share religious beliefs/respect view of others				
60. Common socio-economic goals				
61. Sense of humor				
62. Similar career directions				
63. Accpetance of partner by family				
X. Interdependence/ Equalitarianism				
64. Encourages mutual decision making				
65. Balance between dependence/independence				
66. Ability to rely on others, as well as on self				
67. Ability to enjoy the company of others				
68. Ability to tolerate being alone with no undue stress				

II. PRE-TEST—EVALUATION OF PARTNER

PERSONALITY
QUALITIES

RATING
SCALE

69. Ability to sustain friendships
70. Ability to accept leadership role, as well as subordinate role, when appropriate

outstanding	very good	acceptable	unacceptable

CHAPTER ONE

The Theories Behind Our New Method

In this chapter, we discuss the basic theories that form the foundation of our new method of forming a lasting love relationship. We analyze the feelings of loneliness that afflict so many people, talk about the importance of the childhood experience and demonstrate how it impacts on one's capacity to successfully find a lasting love partner.

Q. *What impact does early childhood development have in forming an adult love relationship?*

Drs. It has tremendous impact. The infant has an instinctive, or at least, very early learned drive to bond or link with the human caretaker who provides nurturance. Most often, the mother is that person, the link to nurturance, to physical and psychological survival.

This need for a link to survival never really completely subsides. The echo, if you will, continues throughout adulthood, with only the caretaker, or the

19

nurturer, changing. As we enter adulthood, there is an intrinsic need to "survive" by establishing a relationship with another human being on a meaningful level. Procreation represents an extension of this survival drive at its most basic level.

The idiosyncratic tendencies of adult relationships have their roots in the manner by which this primary nurturance was provided during infancy. When positive bonding is established during infancy, the foundation for a mature, adult, loving relationship is enhanced; conversely, a disruptive infant-parent situation sows the seeds for future difficulties in establishing a lasting and meaningful relationship. The result? Often, a pervasive sense of loneliness.

Q.   Is loneliness indicative of a basic unfulfilled nurturing?

Drs.   Yes. Loneliness is recognized as one of the most prevalent mental health problems in today's society; consequently, how to cope with loneliness has become a major human endeavor, not only for senior citizens, but for the young adult who is single, because of separation, divorce, the death of a spouse—or simply because he or she couldn't built a lasting love relationship.

Because of the high divorce rate and the single parent family structure, loneliness among adults is pervasive. This loneliness creeps into their lives and prompts a great deal of pain—actual psychic pain—which may ultimately lead to depression. Loneliness then becomes a self-fulfilling cycle, causing an individual to further limit his or her social activities, and diminishing willingness to seek out new significant relationships.

Thus, the person is caught in a quicksand of emotion, struggling with this primitive need to overcome loneliness, yet, losing the enthusiasm necessary to explore new relationships; and, after a point, it leads to depression. This primitive nurturance drive is crucial, and must be satiated.

If depression results, the victim then "deals" with it in inappropriate ways—alcohol, drug abuse, or a series of unhappy sexual relationships. Unfortunately, sex is portrayed in the media as "sine qua non"—the ultimate relief for this pain or loneliness. Of course, such relief is fleeting, just as is the relief provided by alcohol or drugs. Worse, the pain of loneliness intensifies when the person experiences rejection by their sexual partner and the relationship does not evolve beyond the purely physical level. During the absence of sexual contact, the loneliness is particularly painful.

Q. *Would you please describe this process of forming a lasting love relationship?*

Drs. Infants appear to be genetically programmed to respond by learning about, and becoming attached to another person, specifically, the nurturing caretaker; this vital process represents the key to insuring the child's physical, as well as psychological, survival. A natural extrapolation of this concept of attachment indicates that the grown infant—the adult—has this need to maintain such a concept of attachment for his or her psychological survival. And it is precisely this process of attachment which becomes the crucial, primary element in establishing a lasting love relationship.

Consider the infant's attachment to the primary caretaker, often the mother, as life's first loving relationship. If this initial relationship is successful, the infant will have been provided with a foundation on which to establish other relationships as he or she matures.

Later, as the infant becomes an adult, because of that first mother-child relationship being a solid, warming experience, the "programming," if you will, to build a lasting love relationship is stored in one's memory.

Q. You talk about attachment. What, specifically, is it?

Drs. Attachment is an affectionate, loving tie that one person forms with another, which binds the two together in space and endures over time. Attachment is discriminating and specific, and involves affection or love. This is especially true at the mother-infant level. But the method we're introducing utilizes this basic concept to foster adult relationships.

Q. What behavior indicates that attachment has occurred between the infant and mother?

Drs. Attachment is demonstrated by what we call "attachment behavior." Between infants and mothers, this is manifested by the way the mother and baby interrelate—the smiling, the crawling up to, the raising of the arms by the baby, the cooing, the happiness the baby exudes when it's with its mother, and the mother's reciprocal response to the baby. So, the attachment process between mother and infant sustains and nourishes itself.

Q. Are there different kinds of attachment?

Drs. Yes. Attachment can differ in substance and in frequency. The baby can be attached to several caregiving individuals in addition to the primary caregiver, and will respond to these individuals on a gradient scale, being more strongly attached to some than to others.

There is another form of attachment termed bonding, which implies selective attachment with one individual, and, in this book, is used to describe relationships at the adult level. This attachment—bonding—is maintained even when there is no visual contact with the other human being. Between adults, bonding also occurs on an ego level, when a person invests part of him- or herself in the other. We then view this person as vital in what we commonly call a "loving relationship," and this is a focus of the book.

Q. *Attachment . . . bonding . . . how are these concepts incorporated in your new self-help theory?*

Drs. The new method recognizes that in order to sustain a lasting love relationship on an adult level, it's important for adults to have had, in their early childhood, the warm, successful attachment experience we've described. This allows the individual to use that foundation to build a succesful love relationship as an adult.

Conversely, if the attachment experience is lacking or was a negative one, the likelihood of building such a successful relationship as an adult is remote—unless the adult can recognize and correct the situation.

We will introduce a new method to enhance bonding at the adult level for all individuals, but particularly for those who through no fault of their own had less than adequate childhood experiences.

Since we know the infant has an innate ability to form attachments, we're simply interpreting and extending this primitive instinct and interpolating this on an adult level. Often, an individual has no idea how or why he or she is responding to another adult; we will show everyone how to solve these mysteries, and use the knowledge to better their lives—and build a lasting love relationship.

Q.   What about the children of adults already victimized by their inabilities to develop and sustain lasting love relationships- children of single-parent homes?

Drs.   Children of single parents are not being exposed to a complete loving couple relationship. Therefore, the child is not experiencing the process of love and understanding between a couple. This is especially harmful during the first five years of life, when language skills are being accumulated. Then, when the child grows and becomes an adult, there is a lack of this vital millieu that should be stored in his or her memory bank; without this crucial input, the "computer" fails to react properly in loving relationships. This fuels the rising divorce rate.

MY THOUGHTS AND FEELINGS
ABOUT THIS CHAPTER

CHAPTER TWO

What's The (Bad) Attraction?

Too often, the person we're most attracted to is the one who is no good for us. Yet, over and over, we find ourselves dating this "wrong" type of person—never really knowing why, becoming more and more frustrated because of the pain that coincides with the inevitable breakup of the relationship. In this chapter, we will analyze why we sometimes select the "wrong" person—and begin understanding how to correct that.

Drs. If a person utilizes the warmth given him/her as an infant by the primary caretaker, that individual can establish the same quality of bonding with an adult. However, an adult who fails to respond to this new bonding is one who is at this time incapable of forming a bonding relationship because of early deprivation. It does not mean that the person using this method has failed or is being personally rejected by the nonresponsive adult. Therefore, an adult seeking a lasting love relationship should not interpret nonresponse on the part of the other as rejection, and should not fear it. For example, say you try this method with another adult to no avail. If you understand that the individual with whom you're trying to develop a relationship with probably has a deficiency stemming back to early childhood, you need to buttress yourself against a bruised ego or hurt feelings. This approach takes the fear out of establishing relationships. It can remove the shyness on the part of someone initiating the relationship, and shrinks the whole process down to a manageable level. It also takes the self-guilt out of any attempt at a relationship, so that the person making the attempt can overcome the frustration and feelings of personal failures from past, unsuccessful relationships.

A further aid to developing a lasting love relationship is understanding the "copying theory" and using that knowledge to avoid destructive copying of parents in favor of a positive bonding mate.

Q. How does this "copying" process work?

Drs. Consider this actual case history of a 28-year-old female we'll call Jane (not her real name) who has had three significant relationships over the past 10 years. She came to us very upset and crying, because her last relationship ended after a cruise on which her boyfriend had abused her quite severely. She was in the midst of separating from this boyfriend and greatly grieving the loss.

She has many attributes that would attract men. She is an attractive, warm, sincere, intelligent woman whose work involves meeting the public. With those qualities, you'd think she'd have no problem finding the ideal mate. Yet, she chose to be involved in this last relationship, which had lasted approximately eight to ten months, with this man, who, at first, appeared to be her ideal type of person.

Q.   How does the copying theory apply to this situation?

Drs.   To understand that, you first must have some background. Jane had a mother who was an alcoholic. For the first 25 years of her life, her mother was incorrigible. There would be times where Jane—then, just a child—would have to literally lift her mother off the floor and put her to bed. There would be times when she did this for her boyfriend as well. The father was a long-suffering, patient individual who loved his wife and put up with her behavior.

Jane had copied her father's nonsexual personality traits. She identified with her father, who, in this instance was the primary nurturer, so that her personality characteristics were very similar to those of her father, not concerning her femininity, but concerning the remaining traits. Her unconscious method of copying the father was quite evident. For example, Jane was responsible. She always held a good job. She did not drink at all. She was patient. She had great tolerance for stress. She also had a great need to feel in control of relationships.

Jane was not fully aware that she wanted to control situations, until this was pointed out to her. Her father voiced the same kind of feelings, she admitted.

Q.   So, in Jane's case, she copied her father's personality?

Drs.   Yes. But the copying theory goes on to say that while a child will unconsciously copy the nonsexual characteristics of one parent, he or she as an adult will be attracted to and fall in love with a person who has, to a large degree, the characteristics of the "uncopied" parent. So, in this case, Jane copied her father's personality and unconsciously looked for a man who had the same basic personality traits of her mother. Therefore, she was unknowingly attracted to men who had what we call "dependency needs." In this case, alcohol dependency needs.

Q. So, in Jane's life, she is attracted to men who have dependency needs, and not to men who would make good husbands and good mates?

Drs. Exactly. Because of her conditioning as a child and because of this subliminal identifying with her father, she is unconsciously seeking to duplicate the atmosphere that she grew up in; specifically, the relationship between the parents. She is not attempting to duplicate the way they treated her, but how they treated each other. Identifying with one parent forces her to seek someone similar to the other parent, so she can duplicate the atmosphere she was raised in. So, Jane finds herself in this crisis, and can't determine why this situation keeps repeating itself.

Q. Doesn't it seem that we're always attracted to the wrong type?

Drs. If this is the case, it's important to realize this on both an intellectual and emotional level, and that you're able to analyze your romantic inclinations in the terms we just explained. From that point, you can take steps outlined in the book, and clear the way for a relationship based on the bonding concept.

If, by reading this book, you are able to achieve an intellectual and emotional understanding of the forces within you and move into and utilize the bonding principle, then the book is a personal success for you. If, however, the intellectual understanding isn't accompanied by an emotional response—if the reader knows, but can't help himself/herself and is still attracted to the "wrong type," than perhaps this person should consult with a psychotherapist and explore the intellectual and emotional components of their problem.

The book serves different purposes; for some, it may be an introduction to psychotherapy, allowing them to realize that a problem exists, understand why they have the problem and then, through therapy, become masters of this problem.

Q.   You mentioned therapy as one course of treatment beyond this book. Tell us how Jane did under your care.

Drs.   She started to understand her situation and her problems quite well. She went through a period of what we call "mourning," for the loss of the boyfriend, a time she was angry and cried regularly. After a couple of weeks, she emerged from that phase and seemed to be progressing so well that she was considering discontinuing therapy. This normal stage is called "flight into health," and represents a time when the patient still needs further treatment. However, Jane discontinued the sessions and had a date and another disappointment. She dated another dependent man.

Consequently, she became very depressed and entered a second mourning period, which symbolized her letting go of her ideal, dependent boyfriend—the so-called alcoholic type of boyfriend.

This second period differed markedly from the first; the first mourning period resulted from the actual, tangible loss of her boyfriend. The second mourning period was caused by her abandonment of the so-called mother-dependent, alcohol dependent type of man in her personality. An intangible, but still very real loss.

Q. Jane has been attracted to the "wrong" type for all her life. Though she now realizes why she has felt this attraction and has undergone therapy to correct her inclinations, how long will it last? Will she be able to find and fall in love with the right kind of man? Or in a few months, will she find herself back in the same old destructive pattern?

Drs. After therapy, when her understanding is at the correct level emotionally, Jane should emerge from her imprisonment caused by this false idealization. She should be free of her past childhood father-mother relationship.

Q. Will she be able to relate to the bonding theory that you mentioned earlier?

Drs. Hopefully, she would have her new "super structure" in place. Consider her old frame of reference as a house, one which is in need of repair. Now, her unconscious mind has razed that building and cleared a new building site, which is where her new frame of reference will be constructed. This new construction would hopefully house as its foundation her realistic needs for a long lasting relationship not based on that of her mother and father, so that she could utilize the bonding principles described earlier to her benefit.

MY THOUGHTS AND FEELINGS
ABOUT THIS CHAPTER

CHAPTER THREE

How We Choose Our Mates

What role does childhood play in your selection of potential mates? What about how your parents feel toward each other? And toward you? All of these factors play significant roles in how you've come to be the person you are—and also impact heavily on the type of person you select to date. In this chapter, we'll deepen our understanding of this selection process, and continue building the foundation of knowledge you'll need to develop a successful lasting love relationship.

Q. *How do your bonding and copying theories further relate to the type of individual we fall in love with?*

Drs. Let's begin by viewing possible mates as rungs on a ladder. As we proceed down the ladder, we see a group of people that would range from very desirable to a group that would be totally undesirable. We said earlier that depending upon the type of childhood an individual experiences, that individual will or will not be programmed with the ability to realistically relate to other people, to empathize with other people, and be able to become a permanent or long lasting life partner. Now, let's take a closer look at the qualities that make for a long lasting love relationship partner and elaborate upon the mate selection process, paying particular attention to the role of early bonding.

Q. *What examples of good bonding would enhance an individual's capacity to select an appropriate mate?*

Drs. The first six years of life—that time when Freud felt the personality is formed—are crucial. Ideally, a "good mother" (or other primary caretaker) would be competent in many spheres, would be at peace with herself, and be able to give the child proper doses of love, security and independence as the infant grows older. The quality of the bonding principal would be determined by the way the mother holds the baby, the way the mother looks at the baby, the way the mother feels about the baby—consciously and unconsciously— and by the overall establishment of a mutual rapport between the baby and the mother. All these things occur and evolve continuously on a day to-day basis. A mother establishes a good start in life for her baby by accepting the baby's everyday activities as a part of the child's growing, and not as an annoyance. She understands and recognizes stages of development the baby experiences, evaluates the baby's needs and what the baby is capable of actually giving to her at various points in its development.

A mate has to be able to show the benefit of that positive early bonding experience, because that enhances his or her capacity for affection, understanding and love.

Q. What traits can we look for in an adult to determine if this early positive experience occurred?

Drs. What should we look for in a proposed mate? We can judge much about a person by evaluating several factors: his or her background; the type of friends that one has, and the duration of those friendships; the type of employment the individual is engaged in, and the stability of that employment; the self confidence of the individual; his or her ability to be open and to share feelings; to show sensitivity; to accept criticism; to be spontaneous; to exhibit warmth and affection; to be trustworthy; and to show a family orientation. All of these are indications of the degree of personality stability, and will be discussed in depth later in the book. These traits will tell us whether or not a person's infancy was maximized by the mother, allowing the individual to develop self-confidence, tolerance for frustration and an ability to love life and not be unduly pessimistic.

A key question is this: Is the person a "giver" or a "taker"? Invariably, the person with a healthy early bonding experience has the capacity to be a giver and is not a self centered "taker" type of person.

Q. Are you identifying the "taker" type of person as a "narcissistic" individual?

Drs. Yes. The narcissistic, or self-centered, person is typically defined in terms of the taker. Conversely, a giver is a person who has empathy for the other person in his or her life—mainly you.

The narcissistic individual seeks pleasure whenever he or she has the opportunity. Unfortunately, absence of pleasure is often filled through drugs, violence, gambling, sexual gratification, etc., or a variety of other undesirable substitutes. So driven is such a person to satiate his or her pleasure need, that the individual seeks fulfillment indiscriminately; consequently, this person is dangerous to be around because of the self-destructive tendencies that invariably affect not only the individual, but those nearest him/her. Yet, some people seek out such destructive partners over and over again.

Q. What prompts the selection of a narcissistic partner?

Drs. First, let us examine the concept of secondary bonding, which occurs in early infancy when the child seeks a substitute source of comfort in the absence of the primary caregiver. For example, a child may become attached to a blanket; when the mother is out of the room, the blanket becomes the mother's representative. When the mother is not present, the baby cherishes that blanket as a source of comfort, much as an infant sucks a thumb as a substitute for the nipple. The blanket allows the baby to have its mother there even when the mother is not physically present; this works because at this early stage of development the infant is not capable of remembering or conceptualizing the mother. We have extended the Witoker theory of "blanket attachment" by adapting the "social environment" a child is raised in as a "secondary social environmental blanket" that one clings to without realizing it. Later, the grown baby- the adult—seeks to duplicate this social environment. Consequently, if the household is very disruptive and angry, the baby learns to survive in that type of atmosphere; indeed, as an adult, he or she will subconsciously seek out the same type of environment again, or seek partners that the individual can establish this kind of relationship with.

Q. *So, in essence, this secondary environmental blanket is a comfort sought by the adult, even if that particular environmental blanket is not a peaceful one, but is instead filled with stress and strain.*

Drs. The individual is unfortunately programmed to seek it out. He or she feels comfortable only when in an atmosphere of turmoil. Additionally, this person will seek out partners with whom to develop this tumultuous kind of atmosphere. Of course, this is all done subconsciously; still, the individual suffers a great deal.

Q. *This behavior seems similar to the copying theory. Is it?*

Drs. Yes. The copying theory dovetails with Witoker's blanket theory of the comforter. By copying one parent and representing the other with an appropriately identifiable person to marry or establish a relationship with, the individual seeks to duplicate the blanket atmosphere of his or her childhood.

Q. *Can a person who has had a negative early atmosphere correct the subliminal urge to recreate the same turbulent environment as an adult?*

Drs. Firstly, an individual who has constant difficulty in forming and sustaining meaningful, mutually beneficial relationships should understand the principles which fuel his/her self-destructive tendencies. Understanding the problem is the key to solving it.

Q. *Can an unhappy individual, one who has difficulty with relationships, be helped by first understanding the seeds of his/her problem?*

Drs. Yes. Someone who has come from a home filled with conflict suffers twice: first, as a child in the home, in spite of the mind's ability to adjust to and accept the hurtful situation; and second, as an adult seeking to reproduce this hurtful environment. Certainly, by understanding the nature of the problem, the person can begin working toward living better and with a positive reality in mind, rather than living to reproduce the hurtful past and, consequently, prolong the suffering. Understanding is the beginning of solving the problem.

Q. Once we gain insight into our own early learned tendencies and we wish to alter them, how can we choose the mate who would help us? How can a person truly fall in love with someone who is good for him or her, particularly when the individual has never been previously attracted to that type of person?

Drs. By acknowledging the principles of bonding, the copying concept and the secondary blanket already discussed, we realize that in order to fall in love with the "new type of person" an individual must allow all those processes to develop in the relationship with this individual. This takes repeated dating exposure, unlike before, when you might date a nurturing or giving person only once or twice before rejecting him or her in favor of a negative person.

Now, you are going to allow more exposure to this "new type" person to allow the bonding and secondary blanket concepts to develop. Through the new insight gained from this book, you will be able to apply the bonding techniques to get that individual to fall in love with you; as that love develops, your new insight will allow you to accept it.

Allow yourself to date the person repeatedly—15 or 20 times—and develop a new emotional capacity to relate to "the good partner" or "the good bonding person." As a result, a comfort blanket will develop within you after the 15th or 20th date; during the first two or three dates, it never would have had a chance to develop, and you would have rejected that person.

As a result of your new knowledge, when you're exposed to another individual of a positive bonding background and a healthy mental state, you are capable of falling in love with that person, if given enough time or enough dating experiences with that individual. Consequently, someone who may have been initially unattractive to you because of your neurotic needs can now become a productive, long-lasting partner.

MY THOUGHTS AND FEELINGS
ABOUT THIS CHAPTER

CHAPTER FOUR

The Impact Of Society

For many years, society told men that it was fine for them to "sow their wild oats" sexually with women; this caused a contradiction, however, when a man married: now, he was to view his wife as a object of his love, not an outlet for his sexual desires.

The women's liberation movement has spawned a similar contradiction in relationships for women: the new sexual freedom does not coincide with the deeper, more rooted feelings so important in a lasting love relationship.

Q. *How conducive is the climate today for establishing a long lasting love relationship? Has the feminist movement contributed to or detracted from opportunities to establish this kind of relationship?*

Drs. Recently, we spoke with Sue, an unmarried, 31-year-old female who had never established a lasting love relationship. She did experience a relationship that almost resulted in marriage, but it ended because of constant arguing and bickering.

Sue was a very strong-willed, opinionated individual. She questioned the sexual "double standard" that exists between men and women. What she meant, of course, was the fact that women, in the past, had been scorned if they were sexually active with men, but the male has always been encouraged, inadvertently, to "sow his wild oats." Because of the feminist movement, this disparity has come into sharp focus, with the women arguing that the double standard should be abolished, and that both sexes should have equal opportunity to express themselves sexually prior to marriage.

The very fact that man has had society's permission to be sexually active created a formidable obstacle to both sexes to establish a long lasting love relationship built upon a "mutual giving," as in the early mother-infant bonding. For too many years, the man has been told he can view women as sexual objects; yet, after marriage, he was to somehow shift his perception of a woman to that of an equal partner. It just didn't work.

Now, the reverse is happening. The feminist movement is setting up women for the same type of failure as men have experienced in the past. Again, the current message—this time for women—is one of self-gratification rather than mutual satisfaction. This flies in the face of the bonding principle, which is built upon mutual sharing of enjoyment—both persons giving and receiving in equal proportion.

What's important is to establish a bonding relationship, and this may require some acts not totally in sync with the feminist movement; nonetheless, a woman shouldn't feel that the feminist movement would look disparagingly at her because of her actions.

While we are focusing on bonding—copying the mother's and infant's relationship and using the early years of life of the individual to be awakened by the person using the bonding techniques—it's also important to point out this same issue should also be considered by men. It becomes a question of a cultural norm versus individual relationships; the two are different, though related questions.

Q. *So, you're implying that the women's movement may actually build obstacles to establishing a long-lasting relationship?*

Drs. Yes, in the exact same way that the cultural double standard has been a negative influence on men.

Q. *Two wrongs don't make a right?*

Drs. Exactly! The woman we were describing—Sue—had been very promiscuous with men. She felt that she could jump into bed with any male at her whim. Now she is, at 31, dejected and depressed, lacking a significant love relationship. If Sue had utilized the bonding principles, she would have put off sex until at least eight months into the relationship, when a bonding would have been established. Sex could have added an extra dimension to the relationship rather than being an exercise in sexual equality.

Basically, therefore, the man is now beginning to perceive the "woman's libber with equal rights" as an antagonist, rather than the woman whom he is seeking as a partner in a lasting love relationship—a helpmate, an aide, a team player, someone who is an individual in and of herself.

If, instead of perceiving the woman as a potential partner, but rather as a competitor, how can he feel comfortable about developing a bonding relationship? When a child sees a parent as a competitor, he/she feels oppressed, threatened, and suppresses his/her emotions; similar processes take place in adults.

For example, a young teen-aged daughter may become a pretty competitor to her mother, who may really be a beautiful woman in her own right, but not when she compares herself to the beauty of her 16- or 17-year-old daughter. When you have that type of competition between members of the same sex, you can see how antagonistic that relationship can become. On a more subtle, less overt level, a similar antagonism develops between a woman who blindly espouses "equal rights" and her boyfriend. The two become competitive and antagonistic and cannot develop the bonding necessary for a lasting love relationship because such emotions are in direct conflict with those of bonding.

Q. What dangers do a couple face in their relationship if the bonding technique is ignored?

Drs. A couple who doesn't utilize this concept will be at a great disadvantage compared to those who do. By having sex before bonding has occurred, before a genuine relationship has developed, the couple actually injures the relationship. Certainly, there are times when that relationship does bond, in spite of an early sexual relationship. However, it is more likely for bonding to take place when sex is delayed.

Q. Please give us an actual example of what you tell a patient seeking to employ these techniques.

Drs. Recently, Sam, a 27-year-old man, came into the office. At that point, he was at a stage where he was interested in forming a lasting love relationship. In a sequential order during a therapeutic session, we reviewed the concepts of bonding and copying. He was told that women and men often speak different languages, that in a sense, they are taught this from an early age. Men tend to be more practical and down to earth; women are more romantic and interested in flowers, candies and special occasions, such as birthdays, Valentine's Day, picnics and other celebrations. It was crucial for Sam to comprehend this.

Then, we introduced and explained the bonding principles; we noted that he should, in a subtle manner and without verbalizing his intentions, basically follow the same routine a mother does with an infant. Specifically, we suggested this: when he meets a woman, he must spend a considerable amount of time with her. We emphasized the idea of spending time because, after all, that's what a mother does with an infant—she is totally involved with the baby on a daily basis. Consequently, spending time is a very important principle in establishing a lasting love relationship.

Secondly, he should engage in conversation, smiling, and sharing interests with the the woman. In essence, concentrate on pleasant-time activities so there will be mutual eye-gazing and smiling, as well as time spent together.

Thirdly, we suggested that, on their dates, he take her out to eat because, again, this is precisely what the mother does with the baby. Most of a baby's waking time is spent tending to its basic needs, including feeding. So, if the male spends time feeding his date, this would help establish the bonding in the relationship. Furthermore, we explained that women like the traditional candies and other sweets; ice cream, particularly, seems to be a favorite. Desserts seem to be a special treat and represent a specific happy time. For instance, birthday celebrations usually include cake, which has a covering or coating of sugar.

Happy times are associated with sweet things, which is borne out by our references of affection in everyday conversation and in literature and songs, when we call those we love "Sweetheart," "Honey," or "Sweetie." It is well established on some level of the mind that sweetness is associated with affection and love. Therefore, it would be an ideal end-of-the-date treat to stop off for ice cream or the like.

Problems crop up, however, when we study today's socializing patterns, which typically occur at a bar. Instead of the bonding type activities, what's happening here is usually under the strong influence of alcohol or drugs, which lull the person into a sexuality mode, rather than a bonding mode. You have the dancing and the movement of the body in a sexually provocative way, with the alcohol, of course, artificially releasing inhibitions. All this serves as a shortcut into the bedroom and completely bypasses the entire process of bonding. Consequently, the relationship is already off to a shaky start, lacking the solid foundation needed for a serious commitment.

Q.   Would you please elaborate on how you advised Sam?

Drs.   Along with what we've outlined, we spoke about the need for being attractively dressed and well-groomed. These are important parts of the bonding relationship. Additionally, we explained that his manner and attitude would be extremely important. Good manners are very impressive to the opposite sex, both males and females.

We also spoke about kindness. The giving quality

of a person is obviously related to the bonding relationship of a parent and the child. In the first year of
life, the child is completely dependent on the nurturing
parent(s). Typically, the mother is in a giving situation,
and she does this with love and affection. Similarly,
kindess is extremely important; it's akin to love and is
recognized along those lines by the individual receiving
it. Again, it evokes in the adult, from his or her infant
experiences, the warm responses felt toward the mother,
which we call love.

MY THOUGHTS AND FEELINGS
ABOUT THIS CHAPTER

CHAPTER FIVE

Macho Man, Foxy Woman

If you're constantly attracted to the "cool" type of person—the macho man, the foxy lady—and you don't know why, this chapter is of vital importance. We deepen our discussion of the bonding and copying processes to help you understand what fuels the "cool" personality—and why you're attracted to individuals who possess it.

Q. *What about the man or woman who seeks as a mate the "tough chick," or the "fox," or the "macho man"— the "cool" sort of person, one who obviously is not soft or sweet but is rather provocative? What if the person is only attracted to the "wrong" member of the opposite sex? How does this dovetail with the bonding principles?*

Drs. This is a very crucial question. Often, the message that is culturally portrayed is to seek out the person who can provide the "me" type of immediate gratification, rather than the long-lasting bonding with its mutual satisfaction. An individual who is attracted to this type of "instant gratification" person has really not matured. This individual is looking for the unavailable or the unattainable mate—just as he or she sought out instant gratification in the first five years of life. He or she now is attracted to adults who assume this trait of unattainability.

Q.   In this instance, is it possible that the parent of the opposite sex was a non-nurturing, non-bonding parent, a rejecting parent? Can the child-turned adult, because of the copying principle, be doomed to to seek constantly that type of destructive partner?

Drs.   Yes, but the situation is far from hopeless. The individual keeps seeking types of relationships which invariably causes that person anxiety. This individual has been programmed from early infancy to find this kind of hurtful relationship. However, with insight therapy, the individual can be helped to shed this yoke and see the opposite sex in its true light, and not perpetuate a destructive socialization pattern that consistently results in self-hurt.

The woman who is looking for the "macho man," and the man who is seeking the suave, aloof woman are both on a track of self-destruction regarding the bonding process.

Q.   Is it possible for a person to prolong a relationship with a person the individual normally would reject because he or she is too "sweet" and doesn't conform to expectations?

Drs.   Could one work around this inclination toward self-hurt by using the bonding principle with a person who would appear to be of good character and qualities—an individual we would call a "sweet" person? Definitely.

Q. *Let's take the situation further down the lasting love relationship path. Could one grow to love such an individual, though not "stricken" by that person?*

Drs. Yes. In fact, when somebody falls in love immediately with another person, without knowing that person's character or personality, the individual is really setting himself/herself up for disappointment. Again, this conforms with the blanket concept, which implies that the adult seeks to recreate his/her home environment, even if its was cold, rejecting and hostile. The individual throws reason to the wind, replacing sorrow for sweetness and rejection for love. Of course, cold reality leaves him or her with a bleeding and broken heart.

Q. *If someone continues with this habit of establishing poor quality, high-risk relationships, what could be the eventual outcome?*

Drs. Either they are doomed to repeat this cycle—including marriage and divorce—many times over, or they eventually just disregard any serious relationship, saying "I will never get married, I will never have a serious relationship."

This proves unsatisfactory and causes a lonely lifestyle- perhaps a very depressive lifestyle. We're not saying it's impossible to be happy without a partner; however, such happiness is certainly not assured. But since so many men and women are single and have been unsuccessful in finding a mate, people learn how to cope with being single. However, it is preferable, in lifestyle, to have a mate, a bonding partner who will enhance one's quality of life.

MY THOUGHTS AND FEELINGS
ABOUT THIS CHAPTER

CHAPTER SIX

Using The Approach To Change Your Life

How we evaluate others as potential mates carries a great impact on the type of individuals we choose to date. However, it may be necessary—indeed, vital—for some people to change the very process by which they evaluate others. In this chapter, you'll learn how to do that, and how to handle sticky sexual demands.

Q. *I understand how a person establishes a long-lasting love relationship using the bonding technique you introduced, but would you expound on the theory further?*

Drs. Of course. Let's revisit Jane, the 28-year-old woman who had an alcoholic mother and who sought dependent men. The mother's love was the primary love Jane experienced as a child. It was a rejecting love. Consequently, she learned to survive on this counterfeit type of love. Resultingly, she is now programmed as an adult to seek out this kind of love and tries to unconsciously reconcile the problems that beset her childhood by re-creating the same environment in her adult life.

At a recent session, Jane was despondent and sad, and we remarked that she was in such tattered emotional repair. She confirmed our observation, and further explained that she had a miserable New Year's, and was upset. She had recently dated a man a couple of times; in her own words, the individual "put a big rush on her," trying to have sex with her. She strongly resented this and felt cheap. Jane was ready to dismiss this man, even though he did have positive qualities.

We responded by asking her to remember a favorite teacher from school, one who was liked by everyone. She replied that she recalled such a person. We asked if just the opposite were true—that she remembered a teacher the whole class seemed to dislike and had no respect for. Again, she said she did. We then asked her to imagine the same class responding to the teachers differently. We pointed out the situation with this man was similar to the classroom analogy. By rejecting him, Jane is putting an absolute end to a relationship that may turn out to be a valuable type of relationship. But by using the techniques of the experienced, loved teacher—the one the class respected—Jane could transform the relationship into, perhaps, a very significant, long-term one.

We reiterated the bonding techniques and explained about narcissim, a characteristic everybody has to some degree. If she appealed to his narcissism, she could stave off the sexual advances to a later date, when the relationship has solidified—a point maybe six or eight months down the road, after bonding had taken place. Specifically, we advised her that when they were together, she was to be very adoring, very loving, to pay full attention only to him, to use the holding technique, the feeding technique, the looking into the eyes, all the time being very pleasant and respecting. After all, if you embrace theology and believe God is present in everybody, you should be respectful, loving and endearing when you are with any person. Consequently, the person will sense this and be gratified by it. If the feeling on the part of the person—Jane, in this case—is genuine, the receiver of the affection will certainly respond favorably to it.

However, now, she's dating a demanding male, not a dependent one as she had in the past. Armed with her new self-knowledge and understanding of the copying and bonding principles, she can turn this into a possible long-term relationship.

Q.   *How should she handle his sexual overtures?*

Drs.   She should approach his insistence on sexual relations by saying, "Look, I really like you, and I think you're really a terrific person. I want to be with you. But sex is not in the picture, at least not now. You can have sex with 10 other women, but not with me. If you want to go out with me, fine; I would love to have your company. Maybe six or eight months from now, if we're ready to make a commitment to each other, then we can consider sex, but not until then.

"Now, if you want that kind of relationship with me, great; we'll be good companions and friends. If not, call me when you change your thinking and decide you want to date on those terms; if I'm not involved with anyone else, I'll be glad to go out with you again and pick up where we leave off right now." She understood everything we said, and agreed with it; apparently, we provided her with some insight into the male psyche. Jane promised to use these new techniques, and left our office feeling much better. Her depression lifted somewhat, and she did not feel as lonely and miserable as when she had come into the session.

Now, Jane understands her past and what motivated her self destructive behavior. She now realizes the importance of evaluating people—particularly men— for their own self-worth, seeing them in terms of their own qualities: maturity, kindness, love, respect, the capability to fall in love and the capacity to share their life with someone. As a result of counseling, Jane is beginning to understand these things. She does not have to live a second life and repeat the same unfortunate childhood she grew up with. This is one of the great advantages therapy can provide a person.

*MY THOUGHTS AND FEELINGS
ABOUT THIS CHAPTER*

CHAPTER SEVEN

Narcissism: The "I-Me-Mine' Syndrome

To some extent, everyone's personality contains some degree of narcissism; however, when this character flaw is prounounced, it typically dooms a relationship to be a self-destructive one.

Q. *Please elaborate on narcissism, especially since we hear so much about the topic today.*

Drs. Drs. Narcissism was originally written about by Freud, who defined normal narcissism as a stage a child—age two and younger—goes through when he/she considers himself/herself the center of the universe. As the child gets older—past the ages of 2, 3 and 4—he/she realizes he/she is not the center of things, that the world does not turn around him/her. This is the normal psychological course a child would chart. However, if there is upheaval in the family or the child has been mishandled, then the narcissism clings and the child-turned-adult is a very closed, selfish person. He/she still believes that he/she is the most important thing in the world and that the world should turn for himself/herself.

This type of narcissism mandates that the individual must overcome feelings of inadequacy in other areas of life; so, even though the person may behave in a superior way, he/she is plagued by a great deal of underlying inferiority.

The narcissistic person seeks the type of people to relate to and satiate these arrested emotional needs; always the taker, he/she looks for in a mate a person afflicted with an extreme martyr type personality.

If you do not perceive yourself as a low self-esteem, martyr type person who yearns to be servile to a mate, then the narcissistic partner is someone that you should avoid.

Q. Does narcissism stem from a lack of proper nurturance or love from one's parents?

Drs. Yes. That is one origin. Another cause is when the parents are not able to give direction to the child and grant his/her every wish instantly. That translates into an adult behavior pattern of instant gratification, when the individual seeks adults who simply serve him/her. In this instance, the fundamental life experiences manifest themselves negatively in the grown-up adult as narcissism, which, of course, hampers that person's ability to relate to a mate in a loving and bonding manner.

Q. Would a couple—one of whom has narcissistic tendencies—benefit from counseling?

Drs. Yes, even if they are already married, therapy will help them maintain the marriage. If the couple is just beginning to date, to be forewarned is to be forearmed.

Q.   Without such therapy, would such a couple experience difficulty utilizing this technique?

Drs.   Yes; this situation translates into a poor prognosis for a happy marriage. Basically, a narcissistic person is someone with whom you probably would not want to share a relationship.

Q.   What attributes should a man look for in a woman, aside from what he thinks is beautiful and attractive? Similarly, what qualities should a woman look for in a man?

Drs.   Keeping in mind the copying theory and bonding theory that we have already discussed, it's possible to answer the question without regard to gender. A single adult of either sex would really be looking for the same qualities in a potential partner, because there really is no sexual difference between the qualities that one should look for in a mate.

Theoretically, then, both sexes should be looking for the same type of personality factors in the opposite sex, which contradicts earlier philosophies on the topic. In the past, the man was granted the macho role, and the woman was subservient; however, today, we are recognizing that a warm, binding relationship is something that either the female or the male must have in their background for the relationship to work.

MY THOUGHTS AND FEELINGS
ABOUT THIS CHAPTER

CHAPTER EIGHT

Qualities Of The Ideal Mate

We all have an idea of our Prince or Princess Charming, but how realistic is it? Is our concept of the perfect person really perfect for us? In this chapter, you'll discover what key traits contribute to the makeup of the ideal mate . . .

Q. *Please describe the major traits a man and a woman should possess.*

Drs. First, the person we are falling in love with, or are going to fall in love with, would have to be basically a good human being. Admittedly, that is a broad definition, but we could further narrow it to someone who has the capacity to love. Somebody who has warmth, and consideration; somebody who has empathy for you.

Q. *You are suggesting a mate who is a mature individual?*

Drs. Yes. The question many people pose is: where is such a mature individual? Many single individuals are constantly frustrated because they cannot seem to find anyone in that category. But these same people forget about the one person they met who did fall into that category but whom they rejected, either because the person was not good looking enough or appeared to be the type that they are not attracted to.

During psychotherapy, the patient becomes aware he or she has been summarily rejecting mature individuals, and instead has been attempting to develop a relationship with an immature individual, consequently becoming repeatedly frustrated and depressed when the relationship disintegrates.

Many times, a patient—male or female—will say, "Yes, I have had many men or many women like me, but they are not my type." Unfortunately, the type that is their type is invariably the immature or heart-breaking type. So, it's incumbent upon each individual to search into his or her mind and discover the roots of attraction to the difficult potential mate, if that is a problem for an individual.

Q. Please describe the traits of a mature individual.

Drs. A mature individual is somebody who does not consistently behave like the narcissistic person described earlier. The mature individual is able to consider the needs of his or her partner in a realistic way, and derives pleasure from giving to that partner, not just receiving.

A mature individual does not chase a fantasy quest for the movie star as a mate, and does not consider physical attributes as the primary qualities one is seeking.

Q. In other words, physical beauty does not provide the basis for the relationship to be a long-lasting one?

Drs. Yes. In fact, the really physically attractive person would run a risk of being a spoiled individual—perhaps even a narcissistic one—because he or she may have been given things without earning them. As a result, the person can grow up with an unrealistic expectation that things will continue in the same manner during adulthood. In a sense, a spoiled individual has been created just because one happens to be attractive to the eye. That is not to say, certainly, that all attractive people are spoiled.

Another problem associated with the good-looking person is that because he or she is often looked upon as an object of beauty, no one goes further and explores the inner personality. Consequently, the good-looking person has a problem just trying to overcome the stigma we have just described; of course, this stereotype does not apply to all attractive people.

Also, since these individuals are attractive to the opposite sex, they are subject to greater temptation to break their fidelity bonds.

Q. Please further describe the traits of the mature individual.

Drs. The mature individual also is a person who has some type of channel or direction in his or her career. The person is not fantasizing, but is advancing step-by-step toward certain goals. Therefore, if you meet a very nice person in his or her mid-30s who has not fared well in jobs, that would be a sign of immaturity that you should explore.

Additionally, the mature individual has the capacity to enjoy oneself; he or she is happy with oneself and is happy to be on this earth. This individual is capable of enjoying things on a daily basis, and doesn't require fantastic, unlikely events like winning a sweepstakes for happiness. Instead, happiness is derived from such daily events as just enjoying a meal or conversation.

This is clearly contrasted with an immature person, who is a complainer and has a low tolerance for anything that goes wrong. This person's conversation tends to focus on the negative experiences in life, rather than the positive experiences.

Q. *So, the mature individual is optimistic, positive and has good feelings about people and oneself?*

Drs. Correct. For example, the cynic would constitute a personality that represents negative potential for a long-lasting relationship. Conversely, a mature individual has a good sense of humor, wit and certain openness in attitude.

The mature individual is very capable of establishing friendships and will have friends of the same sex for many years; such stability is an excellent indication that one is capable of a long marriage relationship.

MY THOUGHTS AND FEELINGS
ABOUT THIS CHAPTER

CHAPTER NINE:

A Case History

What follows is a verbatim dialogue with a young woman who prospered under our care. As you read through this chapter, you'll note how we talked her through several problems, and helped her to make the self-realizations vital to cultivate an emotional and mental climate for her to build a lasting love relationship.

Drs. What are some of the experiences that prompted your inability to continue a relationship with a man? What personality traits turned you off?

A. Well, most of the men I met were very afraid of making a commitment, and that was real important to me. I don't like to date around. I like to have a stable, steady relationship with one person exclusively, and most men are afraid of that commitment. Many men are also very narcissistic, very oriented toward not staying with one woman, and this makes them less willing to put much into a relationship; they tend to be very selfish, and not very giving.

Drs.   They are just looking for fun?

A.   Exactly.

Drs.   Is it primarily sexual?

A.   Sex is a good part of it, but overall, I had the tendency to meet guys who were self-centered. Sex was a part of it, though; in some relationships, the guy was just with me to try to get me into bed, and the relationship was completely for that purpose.

Drs.   Other men possibly offered more, were more mature, but still lacked something. What is it that they lacked?

A.   Maybe an openness or a lack of getting in touch with their own feelings. A lot of men that I met were more concerned with football or television than talking about their feelings.

Drs.   You're saying that many men are not only out of touch with their feelings, but they may even be afraid to examine their feelings. Do you find that women are more in touch with their feelings?

A.   Yes.

Drs.   What prevents a male from making a commitment to one woman?

A.   A fear of closeness.

Drs.   If you get close, you have to show your feelings, right?

A.   Exactly.

Drs.   So if a man has four or five different women in his life, he's insulated from having to show feelings to any of them. But if he has only one woman, then eventually, feelings will surface in the relationship.

A. Yes. I give myself a lot of credit; I consider myself an intelligent person very in tune with my emotions; as a result, I expect a lot from the person I'm close with— maybe more than other women do.

Drs. What are some of those traits you expect in a man?

A. I want warmth, flexibility, understanding.

Drs. A person who is able to be, let's say, sympathetic or empathetic to your feelings?

A. Empathetic.

Drs. Give us some examples. An excellent way would be to describe your current fiance.

A. This week, I was sick when we were supposed to go out on a date. When I began feeling ill in the car, he drove me right home. I rested in the back of the car, and he kept checking on me the entire trip home. He was concerned. I went to sleep for a while when I got home; while I was sleeping, he had gone out shopping and made me dinner. He just kept checking on me.

Drs. In other words, he was demonstrating a caring— a sincere caring- for your well-being?

A. Yes.

Drs. Do you reciprocate that concern for him?

A. Definitely. Sometimes, I give him things I shouldn't expect in return, like small notes.

Drs.   Would you say that your mother and father behaved similarly toward you and toward each other?

A.   Yes. My parents have a very loving relationship; they have been married for 27 years.

Drs.   What kind of advice do you give a girlfriend who laments, "The kind of guys I'm attracted to are the creeps. The good guy, the one who cares about me and who is nice, I just can't get turned on by him"?

A.   I have experienced that feeling, too. Even now, the part of my boyfriend that I sometimes don't like and question is that occasionally, I'd like him to be more macho than he is. In being so kind and warm, he seems to lack a certain toughness—a toughness that is appealing to me.

Drs.   And that toughness is missing?

A.   Exactly. Because most of his qualities are warm and emotional, and they are considered to be feminine traits.

Drs.   You associate that behavior with the female and consider the male more of a macho, strong, take-charge, domineering type?

A.   Yes.

Drs.   How do you justify your own contradictions? This is a very important point.

A.   The guys I tended to date were the macho, good-looking, tough guys, and the more that I was with them, the more I realized they were not really what I wanted. They were protecting themselves, not me.

Drs.   They were involved with competing with themselves, and not worrying about you?

A.   Exactly. It represented a certain strength to me.

Drs.   And you found that attractive?

A.   Yes, a certain strength appeals to me. You know, I have liberated friends, and I would like to think that I am as liberal as possible, but I still think in a relationship, I need to feel the man is going to teach me something, that I can learn something from him.

Drs.   Now, we've gone around in a circle. You've described a strong, macho male as someone who is appealing because he can protect you. That conjures up an image of an old western movie, with the guys protecting the women from the Indians. That's macho protection. But earlier, you described your fiance as a person who wants to care for you and protect you out of warmth, softness and love.

A.   Yes. I was taught basically, or at least I used to have the idea that a macho man is strong and tough, but, at the point I've now reached through my experiences with men, I've learned what real strength is.

Drs.   But you would like your fiance to be a little more macho.

A.   Yes. That's the sexual part of it. Candidly, my best sexual experiences have been with the guys who are real tough.

Drs.   They place you more sensuously in the female role?

A.   Yes.

Drs.   So, the sexual excitement is generated for you when the man really gets into it on a very aggressive basis, or when it appears he knows what he wants from you?

A. *I like it when he knows what he is doing. I can't say I like aggressive sex.*

Drs. Maybe you just like the image of it before it actually gets down to the act—just the idea of the aggressive male.

A. *Perhaps it's something like this, the man being in control.*

Drs. Then a man who takes charge is attractive to you?

A. *Yes.*

Drs. Maybe what's appealing is the animalistic desire on the part of the male—that a woman likes to feel desire. If you are attracted to someone whom you know is "not giving" and does not have the qualities that you are really looking for, you seem to be almost masochistically attracted to him because he typifies this macho male image and exudes a strong sexual attraction.

A. *I have reached the point where I am able to determine what situations mean to me. For example, before I met my future husband, I was able to get involved in relationships that were purely sexual, simply because I realized that was all it was, and I could appreciate it for that.*

Drs. But you were able to know that you could not engage in a further relationship with this person?

A. *Right, but it took me a long time to get to that point.*

Drs. Prior to reaching that point, you were confusing your desire for the macho guy with the one capable of closeness.

A. *Exactly.*

Drs. Why?

A. *I hoped that I would get married some day and have a wonderful life with a person of that type.*

Drs. And then you discovered what?

A. *I found that type of person wasn't the type that I could marry.*

Drs. Are we really saying that women and men are doomed to have this sexual attraction to someone who is basically a rejecting person—someone who may only be lustful? And that the only alternative is to have a long-lasting relationship with someone who is not as sexually stimulating?

A. *Not at all. I have found happiness by realizing that nothing is ever going to be perfect; I am not going into this relationship saying that everything is perfect, because it is not. As I mentioned before, one of my biggest problems in this relationship will be . . . that while he is a very intelligent person, there is something about the macho part that is missing. However, at this point I am ready to say I am willing to sacrifice that for all the other things. But the only way I got to that point was going through a lot of bad experiences and clarifying my values.*

Drs. You're suggesting sexual excitement comes with a lot of newness- a new man that you meet, one with certain physical qualities, and one who has a narcissistic personality and is rejecting you one way, and seeking you only as a sex object.

A. *It's not that conscious.*

Drs. Many women are attracted to the kind of male I just described, who basically is rejecting of the female. Why is that type of male attractive to the female? Why is that a turn-on? Given two good-looking men, one who is very good looking and sort of sensitive, not one of these narcissistic types and one who is equally good looking, but is the macho kind of guy that we are talking about, women tend to be attracted to the latter type. Why?

A. *Some women, in order to be needed, feel like they have to be dominated and I think it has a lot to do with how women feel about themselves. But it comes back to the feeling of strength and power that the man has.*

Drs. And that makes the woman happy, or serves as a turn-on to the woman?

A. *Yes.*

Drs. Perhaps it has something to do with the animalistic tendencies of the human psyche. In the animal world, the male pursues the female in an aggressive, dominant way. Maybe instinctively, that behavior pattern remains imprinted on the human mind. With our intellect, we appreciate the loving and caring person, but instinctively, the female feels that she needs behavior more aggressive as a turn-on. Such erotic feelings are triggered by the animalistic male.

A. *That's true.*

Drs. It doesn't make sense, but it's there.

A. *I agree.*

Drs. We're faced with a biological, instinctive animal response that causes the aggressive, powerful male to make the female sexually turned on.

A. *Yes.*

Drs. Obviously, modern men and women are in a dilemma, a conflict. One urge is for a mate to possess the animal strength; the other is for the same person to be warm, sensitive and loving. By recognizing this conflict, the female can better sort out her feelings, and similarly, the man can internalize these animalistic tendencies but occasionally act aggressively to satisfy that need in his partner. You would need to communicate this sexual message to your partner.

A. *Yes.*

Drs. When you were younger and looking for a partner, you were attracted to the type of man we just described, a more sexually dominant one. How did you balance that need with the need for a long term relationship?

A. *It's just a question of priority. It's just a matter of priority and having . . .*

Drs. A balance?

A. *Yes.*

Drs. Do you feel that the way you reached this point was by having had those experiences?

A. *Definitely.*

Drs.   And it was painful.

A.   Very, very painful. I really think that I was depressed for a long time just dating; that was about one year ago. I really view myself as a good person, and I just couldn't understand why these people were doing things to me.

Drs.   They were hurting you?

A.   Yes. Then after I realized it wasn't me, and that it was them, well, that's the understanding that you have to come to . . . single women have to realize that it's the man's problem, and not theirs.

Drs.   It's not your inadequacy they are rejecting, but are simply avoiding a close relationship with anyone.

A.   Exactly. I can recall sitting home on New Year's Eve by myself without a date. I wrote in my diary, "you guys are missing out" because they didn't know what they were missing. You just have to be self confident.

Drs.   You're a confident woman, an intelligent professional, and yet these men that we are talking about, these macho men who are strong and aggressive, are afraid of achieving a feeling relationship with a female, a fact which is clinically true. Now why would these macho men be frightened of an intelligent, nice woman like you? Obviously, you must represent something negative to them.

A.   Right.

Drs.   How have they described to you about their attitude toward females?

A.   For example, I went out with one guy for awhile.

He was a young and very successful man, but not looking to make a commitment; he was more happy going to play basketball with the guys, going out with his friends, doing things on his own and was very selfish. I stayed with him for awhile because when we were together we had fun. He had a lot of qualities that I liked.

But a lot of men need and want women who are less intelligent and more subservient than they, and there are many women willing to assume that role. A woman such as myself would like to examine why we do the things we do, and why we seek those kind of men who do not want to put that personal investment into a relationship. They would rather have the wife cook dinner and then be free to do their own thing . . .

Drs. And use you as an object.

A. Yes.

Drs. What can you tell a person to save her from a year or two of painful dating experiences, based on what happened to you?

A. One of the most crucial mistakes was my belief that I would get married and live happily ever after. I came from a close family, and my goal in life was to get married. My parents' marriage was very successful and that is what they wanted for me. What has made me happiest is just realizing that nothing is going to be perfect. In understanding that, I am able to compromise and I am able to realize that I have to work toward something, that is not just going to come; I think that is a real important realization.

Drs. Let's say you met someone who has the strong, domineering sexual attraction, yet, intellectually you realize that he is not capable of a real solid marriage. He comes from a broken home himself and projects an inability to make a real commitment. Would you marry him?

A. *No.*

Drs. Even if you were strongly attracted to him, not just sexually, but in a more pervasive fashion? Would you be able to stop yourself from marrying him?

A. *Yes!*

Drs. Have you ever considered marriage with such a person, thinking that you could change him afterwards?

A. *Yes. That is an excellent observation, a real big lesson I learned. I was going out with a guy for about a year. He was handsome and very good to me. But the relationship was good and bad; I felt that I was teaching him all the time. He owned his own business, and had the potential, and maybe he would be successful, but I did not feel an intellectual connection; as a result, it was a very painful relationship just because he kept pursuing me and I finally put an end to it because I finally realized I didn't respect him.*

Drs. And you backed away?

A. *Yes. I backed away.*

Drs. Was there a time initially when it was a good relationship, when you were really very attracted to him?

A. *Yes. It took me a long time to determine exactly what it was that I was running from. I finally realized what my most important combinations were; that I* *couldn't accept him being macho, handsome and good without feeling that there was a sharing of ideas.*

Drs.   A less mature person may have married that man and wound up divorcing him a few years later.

A.   That's probable.

Drs.   Because you balanced your priorities rather than reacting at an instinctive level, you were able to avoid a terrible experience in your life. This proves that if you base your relationships on just pure instinct, you wind up with nothing but disappointment.

A.   The men in dating circles that I was in, well, they were not derelicts; they were successful, intelligent men and I wasn't going to bars a lot. I was meeting people through friends. I did go through a phase when I went to bars and met people that way. I hate to sound prejudiced against men, but . . .

Drs.   But that's what you were up against.

* * *

The conflict inherent in balancing the needs of men and women revolves around the desire for a loving, caring, warm relationship—which is the mature approach—and the more animalistic feelings of sexuality and lust, which again, the female subliminally desires in a dominating male. The woman is in conflict because her intelligence demands one type of man and her basic primitive instincts is excited by the macho or the dominant type of male, one who is able to ride roughshod over her at times. The male is in a similar conflict in that he wants a woman to be giving, soft and warm, but he simultaneously expects her to be sexually exciting.

Regarding this last interview, we can see that the long lasting love relationship has to take into consideration the animalistic side of human nature as well as the civilization side. This dilemma is one faced by both men and women.

MY THOUGHTS AND FEELINGS ABOUT THIS CHAPTER

CHAPTER TEN

Summing It Up

We now sum up the main tenets of this mew method in a concise, 18-point program which you can use to form a lasting love relationship.

Q. *Doctors, the woman you just interviewed took many years to realize the pattern she was in—seeking the wrong type of macho man. Can insight just happen?*

Drs. If you mean can one realize one's self-defeating behavior in a short time, the answer is yes. However, gaining awareness implies a good deal of inner work.

Q. *What do you mean by this inner work?*

Drs. You must consciously decide to take charge of your life and commit yourself to change. Then the real work begins. You must pay attention to your behavior patterns with the opposite sex and expend a great deal of psychic energy in the process. You will have to battle

with that part of yourself, the more unconscious part
of your personality that is resistant to change.

**Q. Doctors, the woman in the interview realized she
would not find a perfect man. How do you feel about
her decision?**

Drs. She had matured over the years. The bad experiences with domineering, sexually lustful men made
her want to change. In this process, she came to a critical
realization that human beings are not perfect. No one
person can meet our every need or requirement, which
is often rooted in the childhood fables of the perfect
couple—the prince and princess, the happily-ever-after
we're all seeking. Real people have imperfections; that
is part of the human condition. You must accept a member of the opposite sex as a human being and not search
for an idealized Superman or Wonderwoman. Additionally, you should also be aware of the element of
infatuation, which clouds reality and tends to fulfill this
idealized fantasy. We must work to shed the emotional
programs which have been stored in our computer since
childhood.

**Q. Would you please summarize your main points, so
that we have a guide for forming a lasting love relationship?**

Drs.
 1. Early infantile bonding with parents affects our adult
relationships.
 2. Adults attempt to duplicate—to copy—the emotional relationship between their parents in their own lives. This phe-
nomena is explained by the secondary blanket theory and
copying theory.

3. Disruptive relationships with the opposite sex can often be traced to childhood experiences.

4. All adults have the power to make choices. They can establish a long lasting love relationship, even when their childhood experiences of bonding were disruptive and even when they copy the negative qualities in their parent.

5. Adults often establish a pattern in their dating.

6. Key questions to ask oneself regarding long-term relationships include: What qualities do I repeatedly search for in a partner? How do these qualities in the other enhance or interfere with a long lasting relationship?

7. If you experience a series of disruptive relationships, do not feel a pervasive sense of personal failure or rejection. Pay closer attention to the qualities in the persons you get involved with.

8. The emotional "super structure" formed in childhood can be improved. New qualities can be pursued and the old, irrational emotional blanket from the past can be discarded.

9. In falling in love with a "new type of person," we must accept the principle that nobody is perfect. We can shed our idealized image of a mate and replace this illusion with a realistic set of new qualities to actively seek out.

10. Given a healthy bonding potential, a love relationship can develop. "Love at first sight" is often deceptive, and usually hollow.

11. The application of the bonding techniques in our adult lives enhances our ability to establish a long lasting love relationship with a new type of person.

12. We must recognize that human beings have civilized qualities which permit them to be empathic but at the same time recognize that primitive, instinctual sexual urges also impact on human behavior.

13. In selecting a partner for a long-lasting relationship, we

should pay attention to the balance between the needs for warmth and empathy, and these instinctual sexual urges.

14. The cultural standards in our present life combined with our childhood experiences affect our behavior in mate selection.

15. We need to analyze the present and past influences in the selection process. We need to be critical and aware.

16. Two major cultural influence on men and women have been the liberation movement and double standard. Both cultural phenomenon can be obstacles to a long lasting love relationship.

17. Narcissistic individuals make for high risk partners regarding long lasting relationships.

18. A single adult of either sex would need to have the same qualities for them to be a potential long lasting partner. They would have to be mature adults, not narcissistic ones. The capacity for sharing and empathy are paramount qualities in long lasting relationships.

These are the main issues to remember in establishing a long lasting love relationship. It is not easy. It requires a lot of energy and effort. Your capacity for growth will be summoned by our ingredients.

Each of us must continuously work at maintaining the balance. The proportions change as our life circumstances change.

MY THOUGHTS AND FEELINGS ABOUT THIS CHAPTER

Now, it is time to answer the same two questionnaires you did before reading the book. With your new self-knowledge and that of the new method for forming lasting love relationships, your answers may differ significantly from your first set of responses.

Compare the differences, analyzing your answers, in terms of what you've learned in this book. They will help you come to a greater, more comprehensive understanding of yourselfs54and your potential partner.

I. POST-TEST—SELF EVALUATION

PERSONALITY QUALITIES

RATING SCALE

I. Self-Esteem

1. Ability to take a stand on a controversial issue
2. Willingness to take risks and experience possible failure
3. Belief in your potential for success in achieving goals
4. Ability to appreciate your accomplishments without convincing others of your achievements
5. Ability to recognize your strengths
6. Ability to accept limitations
7. Willingness to recognize and strenthen weaknesses
8. Ability to be resilient after failure
9. Degree of self-reliance and self confidence
10. Willingness to seek assistance when necessary
11. Confidence in your decisions
12. Awareness of physical appearance

outstanding	very good	acceptable	unacceptable

I. POST-TEST—SELF EVALUATION

*PERSONALITY
QUALITIES*

*RATING
SCALE*

	outstanding	very good	acceptable	unacceptable

**II. Communication/
Openess**

13. Ability to voice a complaint without feeling self-conscious
14. Ability to accept a complaint without considering it a personal affront
15. Willingess and ability to share feelings and thoughts
16. Ability to display warmth
17. Ability to try new experiences

III. Empathy/Sensitivity

18. Ability to participate in a reciprocal relationship
19. Respect for the needs of others
20. Ability to identify your own views
21. Ability to admit you're wrong
22. Willingness to listen attentively to others and offer feedback
23. Ability to put yourself in the position of another
24. Willingness to accept others as they are, and not try to change their "bad" ways

I. POST-TEST—SELF EVALUATION

PERSONALITY QUALITIES

RATING SCALE

	outstanding	very good	acceptable	unacceptable

IV. Social Responsiveness

25. Accepting responsibility for your own actions
26. Ability to get along with others
27. Social manners
28. Quality of friends of the same sex
29. Acceptance of your social role and responsibility
30. Ability to maintain career goals

V. Control

31. Moderation in general demeanor
32. Ability to accept criticism without losing your temper
33. Self-discipline
34. Ability to delay impulse gratification
35. High tolerance of frustration
36. Capacity to plan for the future

VI. Predominant Mood

37. Ability to work at high-energy levels when necessary
38. Ability to maintain an even disposition/exhibit patience

I. POST-TEST—SELF EVALUATION

PERSONALITY QUALITIES

39. Enthusiasm/spontaneity
40. Predictable behavior patterns
41. Ability to avoid sulking after disappointment

VII. Affection/Sexuality

42. Warmth in sexual expression
43. Enjoy physical touching
44. Enjoy giving sexual satisfaction
45. Enjoy receiving sexual satisfaction
46. Does not rush sexuality
47. Views sexual compatability as important
48. Ability to delay self-gratification

VIII. Trustworthiness

49. Loyalty to family and friends
50. Consistency in fulfilling commitments
51. Ability to keep your word
52. Consider sexual fidelity important
53. Reliable
54. Keeps appointments

RATING SCALE

outstanding	very good	acceptable	unacceptable

I. POST-TEST—SELF EVALUATION

PERSONALITY QUALITIES

RATING SCALE

	outstanding	very good	acceptable	unacceptable

IX. Social Compatability

55. Share recreational interests
56. Share moral beliefs
57. Similar cultural values
58. Ability to strike a balance between work/personal life
59. Share religious beliefs/respect view of others
60. Common socio-economic goals
61. Sense of humor
62. Similar career directions
63. Accpetance of partner by family

X. Interdependence/ Equalitarianism

64. Encourages mutual decision making
65. Balance between dependence/independence
66. Ability to rely on others, as well as on self
67. Ability to enjoy the company of others
68. Ability to tolerate being alone with no undue stress

I. POST-TEST—SELF EVALUATION

PERSONALITY
QUALITIES

RATING
SCALE

outstanding	very good	acceptable	unacceptable

69. Ability to sustain
friendships
70. Ability to accept
leadership role, as well
as subordinate role,
when appropriate

II. POST-TEST—EVALUATION OF PARTNER

PERSONALITY
QUALITIES

RATING
SCALE

I. Self-Esteem

	outstanding	very good	acceptable	unacceptable
1. Ability to take a stand on a controversial issue				
2. Willingness to take risks and experience possible failure				
3. Belief in your potential for success in achieving goals				
4. Ability to appreciate your accomplishments without convincing others of your achievements				
5. Ability to recongize your strengths				
6. Ability to accept limitations				
7. Willingness to recognize and strenthen weaknesses				
8. Ability to be resilient after failure				
9. Degree of self-reliance and self confidence				
10. Willingness to seek assistance when necessary				
11. Confidence in your decisions				
12. Awareness of physical appearance				

II. POST-TEST—EVALUATION OF PARTNER

PERSONALITY QUALITIES

RATING SCALE

	outstanding	very good	acceptable	unacceptable

II. *Communication/ Openess*

13. Ability to voice a complaint without feeling self-conscious

14. Ability to accept a complaint without considering it a personal affront

15. Willingess and ability to share feelings and thoughts

16. Ability to display warmth

17. Ability to try new experiences

III. *Empathy/Sensitivity*

18. Ability to participate in a reciprocal relationship

19. Respect for the needs of others

20. Ability to identify your own views

21. Ability to admit you're wrong

22. Willingness to listen attentively to others and offer feedback

23. Ability to put yourself in the position of another

24. Willingness to accept others as they are, and not try to change their "bad" ways

II. POST-TEST—EVALUATION OF PARTNER

*PERSONALITY
QUALITIES*

*RATING
SCALE*

	outstanding	very good	acceptable	unacceptable
IV. Social Responsiveness				
25. Accepting responsibility for your own actions				
26. Ability to get along with others				
27. Social manners				
28. Quality of friends of the same sex				
29. Acceptance of your social role and responsibility				
30. Ability to maintain career goals				
V. Control				
31. Moderation in general demeanor				
32. Ability to accept criticism without losing your temper				
33. Self-discipline				
34. Ability to delay impulse gratification				
35. High tolerance of frustration				
36. Capacity to plan for the future				
VI. Predominant Mood				
37. Ability to work at high-energy levels when necessary				
38. Ability to maintain an even disposition/exhibit patience				

II. POST-TEST—EVALUATION OF PARTNER

PERSONALITY QUALITIES

RATING SCALE

	outstanding	very good	acceptable	unacceptable
39. Enthusiasm/spontaneity				
40. Predictable behavior patterns				
41. Ability to avoid sulking after disappointment				
VII. *Affection/Sexuality*				
42. Warmth in sexual expression				
43. Enjoy physical touching				
44. Enjoy giving sexual satisfaction				
45. Enjoy receiving sexual satisfaction				
p946. Does not rush sexuality				
47. Views sexual compatability as important				
48. Ability to delay self-gratification				
VIII. *Trustworthiness*				
49. Loyalty to family and friends				
50. Consistency in fulfilling commitments				
51. Ability to keep your word				
52. Consider sexual fidelity important				
53. Reliable				
54. Keeps appointments				

II. POST-TEST—EVALUATION OF PARTNER

PERSONALITY QUALITIES

RATING SCALE

	outstanding	very good	acceptable	unacceptable
IX. Social Compatability				
55. Share recreational interests				
56. Share moral beliefs				
57. Similar cultural values				
58. Ability to strike a balance between work/personal life				
59. Share religious beliefs/respect view of others				
60. Common socio-economic goals				
61. Sense of humor				
62. Similar career directions				
63. Accpetance of partner by family				
X. Interdependence/ Equalitarianism				
64. Encourages mutual decision making				
65. Balance between dependence/independence				
66. Ability to rely on others, as well as on self				
67. Ability to enjoy the company of others				
68. Ability to tolerate being alone with no undue stress				

II. POST-TEST—EVALUATION OF PARTNER

PERSONALITY QUALITIES

RATING SCALE

	outstanding	very good	acceptable	unacceptable
69. Ability to sustain friendships				
70. Ability to accept leadership role, as well as subordinate role, when appropriate				